Can You See Freedom?

and other poems about the importance of interracial and interfaith understanding

By Victoria R. Crosby

Can You See Freedom?

Published by Tender Fire Books

For information contact: TenderFireBooks@gmail.com

Quantity Sales available.
For details contact the publisher at the email address above.

Printed in the United States of America

ISBN: 978-1-7351238-3-7

Title: Can You See Freedom?

Library of Congress
Case # 1-9253121451

101 Independence Avenue
Washington, DC 20559-6000
First Edition: September, 2020

cover photo by Erin Tornatore

~ Dedication ~

As in America Wake Up and 2020 Hindsight, I dedicate this book to my four sons, three grandchildren, and all children of the world, in the fervent hope that we leave you and your children and all future generations, a much healthier world in which to live.

Praise for
Victoria Crosby's Poetry

"La Fuerza Unida has had the privilege of counting for many years with the support, input, and active participation of poet Victoria Crosby who not only has written poems to celebrate diversity and inclusion but also has been a member of our fundraising committee. An extraordinary member of our Glen Cove community."

Alberto Munera,
Executive Director La Fuerza Unida

"I have enjoyed many poetry readings by Victoria Crosby. Her words move you with her strong sense of curiosity, mutual respect, empathy, fairness, justice, and human bonding beyond artificial barriers. A poet for our troubled times."

Rajinderjit K. Singh,
Leader of the Mata Sahib Kaur Sikh Gurdwara

"As a Jewish leader with Hispanic heritage, I always enjoyed Victoria's poetry and find it inclusive of all faiths and cultures."

Cantor Gustavo Gitlin,
Temple Tefereth Israel Glen Cove

"For over a decade Victoria Crosby has voluntarily used her creative genius to grace the annual City of Glen Cove Dr. King Program with an original heartfelt, inspirational poem. As the chairperson of the city's Dr. King Commission, I would like to congratulate Victoria on her latest endeavor and encourage her to continue to speak 'truth to power' in her own unique way. God bless!"

Sheryl Goodine, Chair of the Rev. Dr. Martin
Luther King Jr. Birthday Commission, whose
father, James Davis, marched with MLK

"It is with immeasurable gratitude that I have an opportunity to congratulate Victoria Crosby, Glen Cove's Poet Laureate, for the publishing of what all will find to be an amazing and unprecedented work. Victoria takes the spoken and written word and paints a picture of meaning and hope on the canvas of our imaginations. Her visions are out in front of us but with the lanes and pathways of poetry she grants us opportunity to arrive at the uncharted territory of true meaning in democracy and racial harmony. Blessings on you Victoria! All will benefit from the transcript of your heart that lie on the pages ahead"

Rev. Roger Williams,
First Baptist Church Glen Cove

"Victoria Crosby adds her delightful and reflective humor to so many serious and sober issues that impact all of us.
It is an insightful read from a white allied perspective."

Rev. Gia Lynne Hall
United Methodist Church

"Victoria Crosby's words have inspired our listeners for over 20 years on many different subjects with her poetry. She's so creative and her style is so unique, she is probably the only person who can find a word to rhyme with "orange!"

Shawn Novatt,
Director, 90.3 WHPC www.nccradio.org

"Victoria Crosby's words provide a vivid glimpse of the much forgotten or overlooked historical struggles and achievements of the black community. These poems embody exactly what our community needs to be reminded of the black community's history in America."

Rod Watson,
Former Councilman and Organizer of the Annual
Black History Month Celebration in Glen Cove, NY

Tender Fire Books

www.TenderFireBooks.com

"I disapprove of what you say, but I will defend to the death your right to say it."

- Voltaire

Introduction

I grew up in a small town in the North West of England and until I moved to the culturally diverse City of Glen Cove, NY in 1984, I never had any friends who were not Caucasian. By becoming involved with many different organizations, I learned that although I can never understand or know the true experiences of minorities or people of color, but I can try to express how it must feel to live in this country at this time.

My hope is that this book will entertain and inspire readers to be the change in the world that we so desperately need.

"When you see something that is not right, not fair, not just, you have a moral obligation to say something, to do something."

- John Lewis
Congressman and Civil Rights Leader

Index of Poems

Can You See Freedom

O say can you see Francis Scott Key taking a knee?
It takes a brave soul with lots of self-control
to protect the concept that all people should be
treated with equality in the land of the free,
yet unfortunately, that is not what people see.

It is seen as a protest of the red, white and blue,
but yet is that entirely true?
The words of the poem by Francis Scott Key
were inspired by a battle at Fort McHenry.
A battle for freedom, for the right to be
governed as a democracy.
To be treated equally under the law
is what these athletes are kneeling for.
They have the fortune and the fame,
and they are using the power of their game
to bring forth an issue long overdue,
that there are too many people who
do not have the freedoms and equality
recited in the National Anthem's poetry.

So before you condemn the motives of these men,
look back at our history and remember when,
Rosa Parks sat down defiantly on a bus,
Martin Luther King stood up and marched for all of us.
For the freedom of Americans of all races,
from across the world, from many places,
to have the right to vote, and for education
without regard from which nation
their ancestors came,
or whether their skin color is not all the same.
For us to be, the land of the free
there has to be equal opportunity.

"People don't realize what's really going on in this country. There are a lot things that are going on that are unjust. People aren't being held accountable for. And that's something that needs to change. That's something that this country stands for: freedom, liberty and justice for all."

- Colin Kaepernick

Keeping the Dream Alive

For many years this country has been celebrating
the life of the Rev. Dr. Martin Luther King.
We remember others whose fight
for freedom and equal rights set them apart.
Many years ago Abraham Lincoln's Gettysburg
address first touched the nation's heart.
The assassination of JFK years ago,
to many still seems like yesterday.
He was a president who tried to bring
civil rights to all people in the USA.

We remember Nelson Mandela who fought
for equality in Africa, his home nation.
Malala Yousafzai in Pakistan
fought for the rights of girls' education.
At the UN she spoke so eloquently
of her fight for gender equality.
Basic human rights extend to all races,
religions, gender and creed
and there should be no need to have to fight
for what is at birth a God given right.

But the world will long remember the heroes,
many who fought and died so that we
can work towards the goal
of a world that is open and free.
Free from prejudice and discrimination,
truly a world of "united nations."

For so many years we have been honoring
the works and words of Rev. Dr. Martin Luther King
and all who stand for freedom today
by marching or participating in any way.

You stand with the heroes of the present and past
so someday we can echo his words
"Thank God Almighty, we are Free at Last!"

Empty cup

With hot "Covfefe"

photos of cups available at

The Unemployed Philosophers Guild
www.philosophersguild.com

On Being Black

"I cannot breathe" Eric Garner cried
as he was held in a chokehold until he died.
"I cannot breathe" George Floyd was heard to say
as they knelt on his neck until he passed away.
These lynchings are happening still
like what happened years ago to Emmet Till.

They are no different than hangings that took place
by the Ku Klux Klan who would hide their face.
Breonna Taylor, an African American EMT,
was murdered in her own home most brutally
in Louisville, Kentucky,
when police entered the house in the middle of the night
and her boyfriend was awakened in fright.
Kenneth Walker, was shot as he tried
to prevent the police from coming inside.
But it was the wrong house into which they had stormed,
and the opinion they had formed
was that there were drugs,
but there were none to be found there at all,
no illegal substances large or small.

The police are supposed to serve and protect
no matter what crime the alleged suspect
is accused of committing.
The police should behave in a manner befitting
an officer of the law
treating people with respect, and what is more,
innocent until proven guilty, is a human right
for people, both black and white.

Breonna Taylor

Eric Garner

George Floyd

Divine Right?

The churches are not #45's personal property
although he seems to think they ought to be.
Tear gas and rubber bullets were used
as peaceful protesters were abused
in order to clear a path for #45 to go
and put on another "reality show."

The Bishop of St John's Episcopal Church in DC
said that it was a surprise, and she,
Mariann Budde, wasn't asked or notified
and priests were tear gassed as they sat outside.
Bishop Michael Curry said #45 could have
asked people to pray
for everyone's health and safety on that day,
and could have asked for prayers for healing,
acknowledging the anger that they all are feeling.
Instead #45 used the church and bible as props
in another of his many photo ops.

"When fascism comes to America it will be
wrapped in the flag
and carrying the cross."*
These words by James Waterman Wise
should make the country realize
that fascism did indeed arrive
in the form of #45.

*Also attributed to Sinclair Lewis and paraphrased by many

"*Everything he (tRump) has said and done is to inflame violence.*"

The Rector of St John's Episcopal Church in Washington DC

Skin Deep

If a person is jogging, who happens to be Black,
does that justify a vicious attack?
They claim he was trespassing on private property,
but does that mean he deserves a death penalty?

Ahmaud Arbery, Trayvon Martin,
to name a few people of color who
were shot by white people on the street,
like the slavery era in repeat,
for no other reason than the color of their skin,
as this country is destroyed from within.

During the recent protests and nights of unrest,
what began as peaceful demonstrations,
and an outlet for their frustrations
over the senseless deaths of so many minorities
has morphed into riotous opportunities.
With bricks the protesters were supplied,
so they could smash windows and steal the goods inside.

Not all police are bad, not all people are good,
There are good and bad people in every neighborhood.
In every ethnic group and nationality you will find
some people who are mean, and some who are kind,
While some police have been brutal, it is true,
some who took a knee in solidarity,
and joined the protest, were men and women in blue.

Twittler

All over the world and in Washington DC
people have been infuriated by what they see.
As enraged citizens march to demonstrate
that they have had enough of hate
towards people of color and minorities,
who were murdered by authorities.

During the time this was going on
nobody could find Don the Con,
as #45 was known to hunker
down inside the White House bunker
during riots which were instigated
by white supremacists, and created
to incite his racists followers on the far right.

There are many who want to compare
#45 to Hitler hiding there,
and hoped that he'd do the same thing while inside,
swallow a pill filled with cyanide.

"...I was there for a tiny, short little period of time... They said it would be a good time to go down, take a look, because maybe some time you're going to need it..."

Donald Trump on hiding in the bunker

On Being A Liberal

What is a Liberal I'd like to know?
To me it refers to people who show
compassion and empathy,
people who practice equality
in their lives every day.
Some people have been known to say
that I have a bleeding heart.
I would rather be that, than a person who
tries to suppress another's freedom and happiness.
There are some people I have heard,
who use Liberal as an insult, an epithet,
a dirty word; and yet,
liberation means freedom,
as in the Statue of Liberty,
from the root word in Latin,
pertaining to a person who is free.

"If by a "Liberal" they mean someone who looks ahead and not behind, someone who welcomes new ideas without rigid reactions, someone who cares about the welfare of the people-their health, their housing, their schools, their jobs, their civil rights and their civil liberties-someone who believes we can break through the stalemate and suspicions that grip us in our policies abroad, if that is what they mean by a "Liberal", then I'm proud to say I'm a "Liberal."

- John Fitzgerald Kennedy

Justin Time

Justin Trudeau's twenty-one second long pause
answered more than the question, because,
Canadians, and the world, are horrified
by what is going on inside
every state in the US nation.
"We watch in horror and consternation."
Now is the time for conversation
on how this issue should be addressed.
Many countries have been blessed
with leaders who rise to a leadership role,
and who actually respond as a leader should,
to work together for the common good,
who put their country before their need
and lustful desire of greed and power.
This is NOT our country's "finest hour."

"We all watch in horror and consternation, what's going on in the United States It is a time to pull people together, but it is a time to listen it is a time to learn what injustices continue ---despite progress of years and decades."

Justin Trudeau after a twenty one second pause before answering a question about Donald Trump's action in regard to Black Lives Matter

Stormy

tRump is so filled with jealousy and hate
that he tried to create
a false conspiracy called Obama Gate.
Now #45 has the White House surrounded
by a barriers and fence
to protect himself and Mike Pence
from the hordes of angry protesters
who might storm the place,
like the storming of the Bastille years ago in France,
tRump doesn't want to take the chance
that American citizens, who are feeling very mean,
and some would say justified,
may want to set up a guillotine outside!

The Enemy of The People

When a president who has sworn an oath
to protect the people, and is both
a traitor and an instigator,
who threatens to use military force
against those he has declared to be
the enemy, of course
he should be removed from office right away.
Doesn't the twenty-fifth amendment say
that a president who behaves in this way
can be relieved of his position,
as he is encouraging sedition?
He must be removed A.S.A.P.
so that the people can be free,
and the kids in cages get their liberty.
and Black Lives Matter becomes a reality.

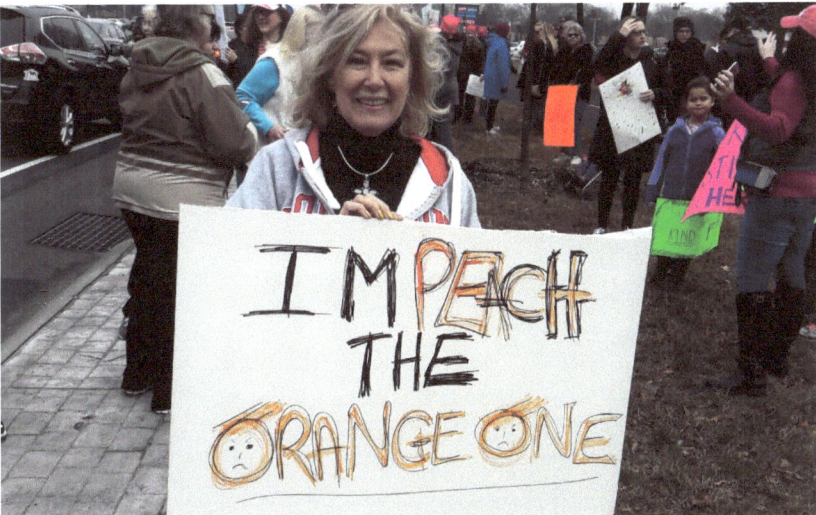

Fulfilling the Dream of Martin Luther King

Over many years people have been trying to fulfill
Martin Luther King's dreams, and to instill
the hope of a better future for everyone,
we cannot rest until this is done.
We must realize the dreams of prophets who foresaw
an end to prejudice and war.
Several students many years ago
sat at a lunch counter, even though
they knew it was futile to expect
to be treated with dignity and respect,
and to order each one a plate of food.
They were ignored and their treatment was very rude.
They knew what they asked was a human right,
but they were refused because they were not white.
Their actions and those of others
who realize we are all sisters and brothers,
helped to bring about a change of law,
but we must not forget how it was before.
It takes a village, a city, a nation,
to bring about change through dedication.
The seeds of change started with a few,
let them continue with me and you.
Let us all pledge here today
to visualize a better way,
A future that will bring
the fulfilled dream of Martin Luther King.

MARTIN LUTHER KING JR.
JAN. 15, 1929 — APR. 4, 1968
FOUNDING PRESIDENT
SOUTHERN CHRISTIAN LEADERSHIP CONFERENCE
THEY SAID ONE TO ANOTHER...
BEHOLD HERE COMETH THE DREAMER...
LET US SLAY HIM...
AND WE SHALL SEE WHAT WILL BECOME OF HIS DREAMS
GENESIS 37:19-20
RALPH DAVID ABERNATHY, PRESIDENT

Chauvinism

Derek Chauvin is the name
of the man who is to blame
for George Floyd's suffocation
in spite of his protestations
for more than eight minutes
on his neck he was kneeling
until George lost all feeling
that he couldn't breath
while other officers just stood around
as George lay dying on the ground
until he couldn't take another breath
and finally succumbed to death.

Chauvinism means feeling better than others,
not accepting all people as our sisters and brothers.
It's derived from the name of Nicolas Chauvin,
who obviously wasn't a very nice man.
He was a soldier of Napoleon's army,
who, like Napoleon, thought himself superior,
but really was just barmy.

Could the two men be related in some weird way?
I suppose it is really hard to say without a test of DNA.
But no matter the relationship or their name
one fact remains the same
they will both go down in history
for actions of negativity.

Equality, Justice and Diversity

In a world where people are attacked
for expressing their views,
the horror stories we hear
every day in the news
of women and young girls
beaten and raped,
or shot because they speak out
to protest their fate,
of innocent children and teachers
gunned down,
attacks in the movies
and on trains underground.

There is no reason or sense to be found.
Where is equality and justice now?
The challenge for us lies in how
we approach these problems
that we face everyday
by standing firm
and not running away.

By following the example
of Martin Luther King,
non-violent protest will help us to bring
an end to violence and hatred,
and replace people's tears
with hope for a better future in the coming years.

Over one hundred fifty years ago
the emancipation proclamation was set forth,
which tried to unite the South and the North.

In every town the diversity of the community,
living together in harmony,
exemplifies Martin Luther King's dream,
so let us now try to live this theme,
not just for today
but to meet the challenge in every way
with **Equality, Justice, and Diversity.**

The Ultimate Price

The death penalty isn't justified
if you tried to sleep off a few drinks in your car,
or sell cigarettes on the street,
but if you do, you may meet
a very tragic end.

Your demise may come my friend,
if you try to pass a small forged bill,
or walk wearing a hoodie on your head,
you could very well end up dead.

Black people and other minority races
have to be very careful of the places
they go, and what they wear,
and they must take care
of how they drive, or they might be pulled over
and not make it out alive.

Black children should never play with toy guns
as they could be mistaken for real ones.
Too many young children have been shot
reaching into a pocket, when all they had got
was a bag of candy, or harmless toys.
Too many mothers have cried for their boys.

Unless you're very famous and wealthy,
like MJ and OJ,
you will not get away with crimes you may
have committed,
and the ultimate price you will pay,
for far lesser crimes than they.

Good Cop Bad Cop

Although there may be more good cops than bad
it makes me terribly sad
to know that police brutality
is still a reality.
Beatings for the slightest infraction,
no wonder there has been a strong reaction.
There is only so much that people can take
before they reach the point that they break.
Screaming, yelling, and throwing things,
in an attempt to bring
attention to what is wrong with society today.
Too much pressure leads to explosion,
a meltdown, a break down, an erosion
of the community,
which leads to greater opportunity
for actions that can end in tragedy.
When suffragettes were on hunger strikes
for the right to vote,
they were force fed by a tube
pushed down their throat.
Some were beaten and taken to jail
where they remained,
as some chained themselves to a rail.
Years later when women demanded equality,
they were still not treated with dignity.
Some would protest by burning their bras,
and others would set fire to cars.
Many have died to win these fights,
including the demands for Civil Rights.
And it's been that way with many a cause,
that violence, destruction and breaking laws
seem to be the only way to get through

to those who have the power to
make the changes that need to take place,
and although it seems a terrible disgrace
that this cannot be done peacefully,
it is the way it's been done historically.
I'm not excusing or justifying
looting and shooting, I'm just trying
to understand how it must feel to be oppressed,
while all the rest tell you that you are free,
that doesn't seem like freedom to me.

"When they start looting,

we start shooting."

- Donald tRump

Inside & Outside

While the pandemic was still raging
#45 was staging another reality show,
at a rally in Oklahoma
crowds of his supporters gathered outside
filling the streets with litter,
showing no sense of pride.
A woman wearing a tee-shirt that said,
"I can't breathe,"
was arrested, handcuffed, and forced to leave.
Police said trespassing was her crime,
but she had a ticket and thought everything was fine.
Sheila Buck was her name,
she told reporters that she came
to the rally to protest peacefully.
She is an American Citizen and she
lives in Tulsa, and what is more

she has never been arrested before.
What happened to her constitutional right
to protest peacefully without a fight?
I am sick and tired of the "crapo"
perpetrated by #45's Gestapo.
Hired mercenaries, owned by none other
than Betsy DeVos's brother.
These "soldiers" who have created such a mess
are the American SS.
Sent for "law and order" to restore,
yet peaceful protesters have no need for
armed goons who kidnap in unmarked vehicles
then disappear.
Their goal is to create a climate of fear.
This is how Hitler took power day by day,
slowly stealing freedoms away.
Martial law has been instated,
and the constitution decimated.

There Needs to be Deeds

In honoring the legacy of the Rev. Dr. Martin Luther King
we have to do more than march and sing.
There has to be more than walking the walk.
There has to be more than talking the talk.
There needs to be deeds.
Feeding the hungry, clothing the naked,
visiting the sick and incarcerated,
these are the actions of love most sacred.
By reaching out to those who have less,
we also increase our own happiness.
Transforming dreams into action
can give great satisfaction.
There needs to be deeds.
Dr. King dreamed of equality
from prejudice and bigotry,
for people of every color from every nation.
That was the basis and foundation
of his religious philosophy.
A dream is wishful thinking and cannot be
turned into reality
unless some action is taken.
There needs to be deeds.
We cannot allow the despots, dictators
and political traitors,
to fuel the fires of hated and derision,
of racism, homophobia and antisemitism.
We must continue to resist
the vile agendas of misogynists.
There needs to be deeds.

"Injustice anywhere, is a threat to injustice everywhere"
is what I have read that Dr. King said.
And that darkness and hate are only conquered
by light and love.
Let us be the light and love that
Dr. King spoke of.
There needs to be deeds!

*Volunteers delivering food, supplies,
and making masks for those in need.*

No Words
of Wisdom

Presidents in the past have made speeches that inspire,
but the present White House resident liar
only attacks and incites sedition,
and if there was a first edition
of all the stupid words that a president has said
or were written or tweeted,
while on the commode he was seated,
#45 would be the winner without a doubt,
and he would be totally left out
if there were a book of every smart words
that past presidents have said,
tRump hasn't said one yet,
at least as far as I have read.
At his rally in Tulsa he had to mention
that his cautious descent down
the ramp was his intention,
and explain that down a ramp he can go.
As his
daughter- in-law said,
"It doesn't have any
steps you know!"
He thinks he's the
smartest in the land
as he can now drink
water from a glass in
one hand,
he doesn't need both
hands like before,
and he doesn't need a
sippy cup anymore.

Covid Rally

They held a rally for #45
I wonder how many will end up alive?
Very few masks were worn in there,
everyone breathing the germ laden air.
Six of the rally workers tested positive
but #45 doesn't give
a damn, and refused to cancel, even though
Tulsa leaders had advised him so.
The temperature outside was 90° Fahrenheit
the IQ of those inside was quite
a bit lower than that.
#45 has said he loves the uneducated,
and obviously those who are medicated.
Maybe they were all injected
with bleach so they don't get infected.
On Craig's List #45 had placed an ad,
as he needed people really bad.
He asked for actors who would attend
the rally, and pretend
to be supporters of his,
to be paid for this job in "show biz."
This gig asked for actors who
would hold up signs and cheer on cue.
There were plenty of seats that were empty,
but social distancing was not observed
and people gathered together didn't seem perturbed.
They drank the Kool-Aid, it's plain to see
as they look like zombies on TV.

Juneteenth

On September 22, 1862, Abraham Lincoln
signed the declaration
freeing all slaves with emancipation.
At that time many slaves couldn't read and write,
to learn was a crime, masters could punish with
beatings of great might,
or even death could be their fate, so it was a bit late
when slaves finally got the news that they were free
and could embrace liberty.
The proclamation read that on January 1st 1863
that all slaves of the confederacy
shall be "thenceforward and forever free."
It was on June 19th 1865 when the news broke through
that slaves were free to do whatever they wanted to.
The news had spread slowly from plantations in the South
to the other states by word of mouth.
It took over two years to reach the Lone Star State.
So now all Black people celebrate
Juneteenth as the day when they could
say "Free at last."
Yet in all these years that have passed
there are too any things that haven't changed at all,
and everybody must heed the call,
for no people can be free,
while others are denied their liberty.

In The Corner

Like a cornered rat he will behave,
seeking only for his own skin to save.
A defeated tRump is dangerous indeed,
and past warnings we should heed.
He is vindictive and will look to repay
those who he feels have wronged him,
and stood in his way;
like Michael Cohen, John Bolton
and Mary Trump, his niece,
they have all written books and said their piece.
Their books he will try to block,
but it will come as no shock,
to those of us who his character,
or lack thereof, is well known,
as he has shown
to be lacking in compassion and empathy
and will be vengeful, you will see.
It is frightening to think
that he had brought us to the brink
of world war three before,
and holds the codes and key
to destroy us all ultimately.
So let's hope that he meets the end he deserves,
and that the time in prison he serves

will be much longer than
his term as liar
in chief,
and that he pays
for causing the
country such grief.

The Joker

The racist term #45 chose to use
to depict the deadly virus, lit a fuse
as the crowd cheered when he said "Kung Flu."
His staff said he was joking,
but I don't think it's funny, do you?
He told the press he doesn't make jokes,
so he really meant to offend some folks
in order to please his twisted base,
which he thinks will help him
to win the presidential race.
He's made fun of minorities,
women and the disabled.

His lack of empathy has enabled
Neo Nazis and the Ku Klux Klan
to display their swastikas and to plan
for public demonstrations and to incite
people into frenzied riots and fights.

He supports dead generals of the confederacy,
but not troops fighting for democracy.
He doesn't want racist statues to be removed,
yet he hasn't said that he disapproved
when he was told by American feds
that Russia had put a bounty on soldiers' heads.

He denies that he was given the intel,
but of course, we all know very well
that #45 doesn't read or listen to any information
that would improve his communication.
What a betrayal for the families of the dead to bear
knowing that their government, "just doesn't care."

Bang Bang

Patricia McCloskey pointed a loaded gun at people
who were protesting peacefully
standing next to her husband Mark, who was seen
pointing a loaded AR-15,
with their fingers on the trigger, which wasn't very nice.

Some years ago a young Black boy, Tamir Rice,
holding a gun that was just a toy,
was shot by police within a few seconds of their arrival,
the twelve-year old kid had no chance of survival.

McCloskey is a lawyer in Missouri,
and is on the board of ethics there.
The fact that she lacks ethics the board
members don't seem to care.
They weren't in any danger
from the group of strangers
who were carrying signs
that asked for justice and peace.

It doesn't seem to make much sense
that she faced no consequence
for threatening harm,
yet the boy who was unarmed
was shot dead without any thought.
Don't you think that McCloskey ought
to be given a fine at the very least
preferably disbarred, should be the plan
as she is probably a card
carrying member of the Klan.

"What you saw happened to us could easily happen to any of you."

"No matter where you live, your family will not be safe in the radical Democrats' America."

-Patricia McCloskey at RNC

Overcoming the Challenges to the Dream

What would Martin Luther King think or say
about the turmoil in the world today?
In a world where terrorist actions are displayed
on the Internet and TV and portrayed
in every newspaper for all to see.
Where children are not cherished as they should be,
but traded like a commodity.
Jesus said, "Let the little children come to me,"
not send them back to where they were before,
back to countries with poverty, gang violence and war.
What would Martin do about the
ISIS crisis and racial tension
that seems to be growing in a world that is showing
a lack of tolerance, respect and understanding
for other cultures, while demanding
attention in media worldwide.
Martin's dream of people living in peace and unity
now seems to be even further from reality.
There is disease and pestilence, weather extremes,
pollution in the oceans, rivers and streams.
And some believe it is the end of days;
or is it an opportunity to change our ways?
"Turn the other cheek," Jesus said,
and non-violent protest was the way Martin led.
Religious leaders ask peace loving people of every nation
to turn to prayer and peaceful demonstration.
And that is what Martin Luther King would say
if he were here with us today.
We must work together as a team
to overcome the challenges to the dream.

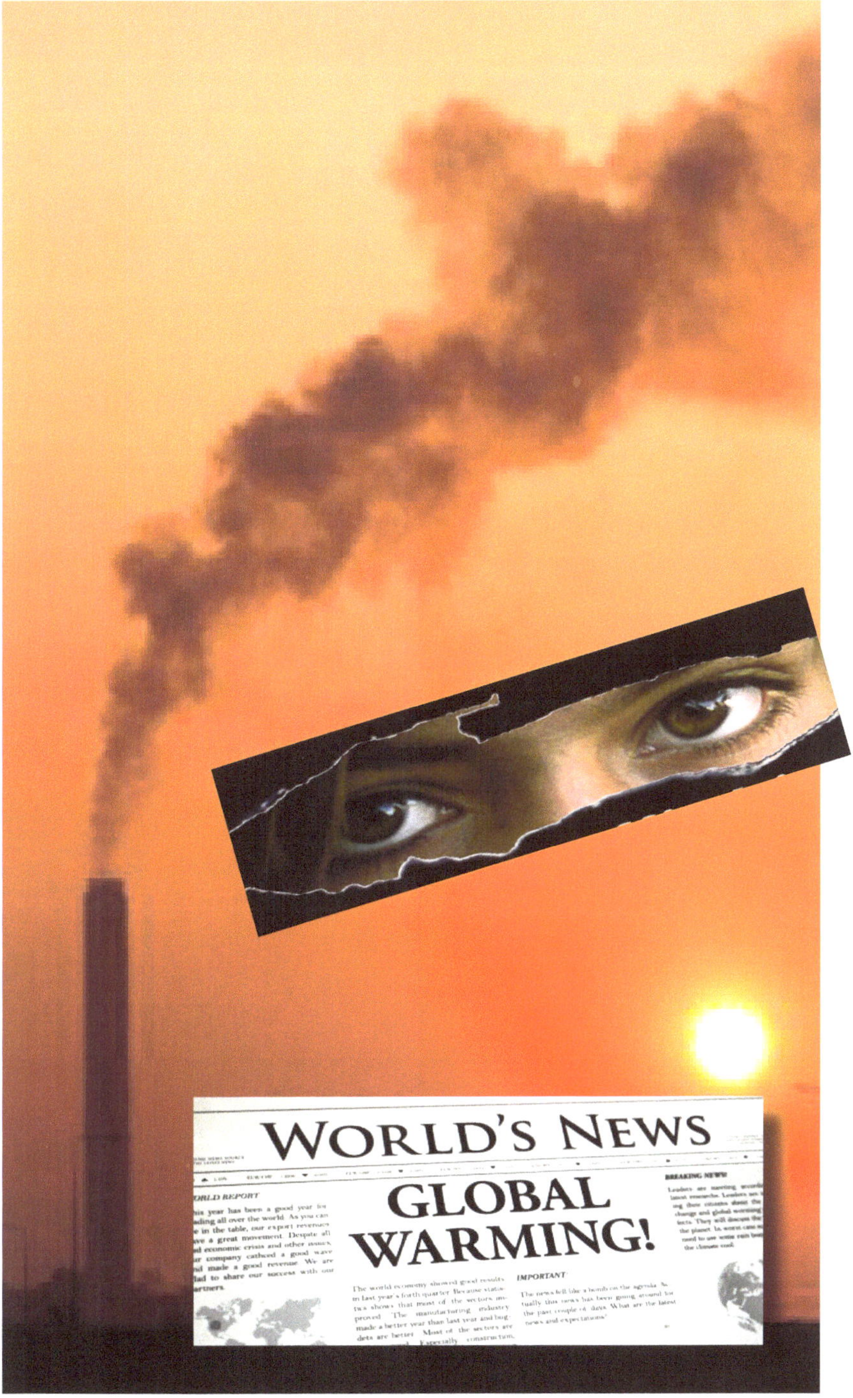
WORLD'S NEWS
GLOBAL WARMING!
IMPORTANT

BodyCam Scam

How many times have people spoken
to say that our justice system is broken.
If you are rich you can get away
with pretty much any crime today,
but if you are a person of color and poor
it's a long jail sentence they'll be looking for.
Too many innocent people are locked away,
while the guilty walk the streets each day.
The prison system doesn't rehabilitate
it's a for profit venture to facilitate.
Sometimes you're lucky if you end up in jail
as our justice system has been known to fail.
The minority community
has suffered too many acts of impunity.
Unarmed citizens have been known to die
for minor infractions
by racist police over reactions.

Elijah McClain, a twenty-three year old man-child
an innocent soul, gentle and mild.
No-one could be further from a threat,
minding his own business, and yet
with a heavy dose of ketomine he was injected,
just because someone suspected
that he was behaving is a strange way
as he was walking home that day.
The drug they used was one
that is often used by vets
to subdue and calm anxious pets.
Like the animals at the shelter
where Elijah played his violin
to sooth all animals there within.

He was just dancing, he tried to explain,
but they put him in handcuffs to restrain,
and in a carotid hold on his neck and chest.
Elijah couldn't breath and went into cardiac arrest.
At a violin performance in his memory,
tear gas was aimed at the crowd
who had gathered peacefully.
There certainly needs to be
training for sensitivity
among the members of the police force,
which starts with the leadership at the top of course.
I'm not saying that every cop is bad, or every person,
whether black or white is good,
but it certainly would help if every cop would
have a bodycam that's turned on and working well,
so if there's a problem, we can tell.

Mary, Mary

Mary Trump a has written a book
that gives a family member's look
into the psychology of her Uncle Don
who she says has been a psycho from early on.
Of course we don't need a Phd.,
to know that she is speaking truthfully,
as from his behavior it is plain to see,
that he hasn't matured since the age of three.

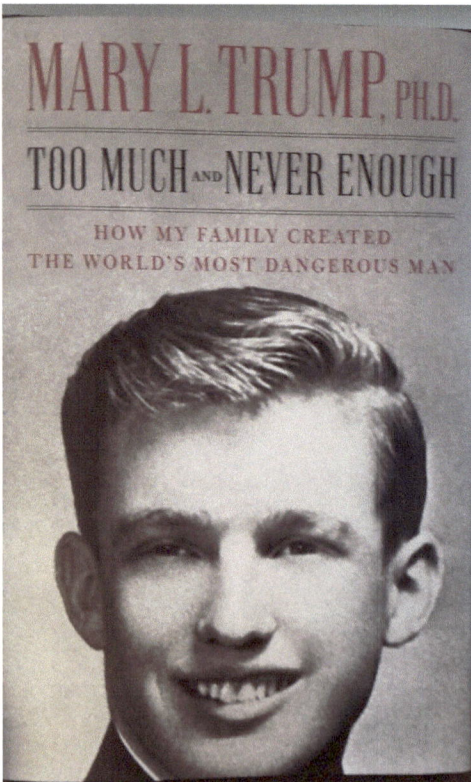

His father was a
tyrant, his mother
wasn't well,
and his brother, Fred
Jr. Mary's dad,
the family put
through hell.

Mary's a psychologist,
who tries to explain
the root of Donald's
problems
which still remain.
His ego won't allow
him to go for therapy,
although he needs it
desperately.

We Are Now Ruthless

Born in Brooklyn in 1933,
Ruth Bader Ginsburg,
a woman of integrity,
left us a wonderful legacy.
She fought for freedom and equality.
A champion for women's rights
she never gave up the fight
battling cancer four times until her demise,
a much appreciated sacrifice.
At Harvard and Columbia she studied law
improving everyone's lives was what she stood for.
As a Jewish woman she found it hard to get hired,
but she never gave up and never retired.
Rights for woman and justice for all
is what Ginsburg tirelessly fought,
before becoming a member of the nation's highest court.
Ruth Bader Ginsburg
will forever be
known as the
"Notorious RBG"
immortalized by Kate
McKinnon on TV.
Not a corporate raider,
but "a robed crusader,
a real-life superhero, a
warrior for justice who
saved the day,"
is what McKinnon
had to say.
A role model for
females everywhere,
an inspiration
beyond compare.

Shoulder to Shoulder

Shoulder to shoulder they marched long ago
to bring forth a freedom that they did not know,
a nonviolent expression of fighting segregation,
to demand equality throughout the nation.
Shoulder to shoulder Martin Luther King walked along
singing a call to freedom song,
with his friends and family at his side,
and the thousands of people who marched and cried
with this great leader, and heard the words that he wrote
as he spoke of freedoms and the right to vote.
Shoulder to shoulder and side by side
for many years we have tried
to be a model community
of diversity and harmony,
by celebrating the anniversary of his birth
and honoring his achievements on this earth.

Shoulder to shoulder we marched today
to continue the legacy and pave the way
for a future generation, that they not forget
the dream and the vision of those who were met
with anger and hatred and hostility,
while marching with grace and dignity.
Although many years have come and gone
hold your head up high, the dream lives on.
to eliminate prejudice and segregation
the legacy is passed to each new generation
and so we hope it will continue to be
a tradition we embrace in every community.

"Never, ever be afraid to make some noise

and get in good trouble, necessary trouble."
-John Lewis

Black History

America is a country of immigrants,
a melting pot, except of course
for the people whose ancestors were brought here by force.
From slavery to freedom great strides have been made,
yet for this progress, a great price has been paid.
And history seems to have forsaken
the indigenous people from whom this land was taken.
As we celebrate and honor the accomplishments
of the great African Americans
who are artists and activists,
doctors and scientists, dancers, inventors and politicians,
astronauts, athletes and mathematicians.
Mae Jamison was the first Black female astronaut who flew
in The Endeavour in 1992.
Rosa Parks, MLK,
Maya Angelou, and Sidney Poitier.
Poets and writers, and the Harlem Hell Fighters.
Television actors and movie stars,
with Hollywood mansions and exotic cars.
Celebrities like Oprah and Denzel,
who make us feel that we know them well.
Madame Walker, and Annie Malone,
were both Black women who made fortunes of their own
Arthur Ashe, Malcolm X, and Queen Latifa,
Ashanti, Wendy Williams, Venus and Serena.
Tuskegee Airmen and players of sports
on football fields and basketball courts.
Ballerina Misty Copeland, who in 2015
was one of the 100 Most Influential
People in Time Magazine.
President Obama, Andre Watts, Beyonce and Ben E King,
and so many more Black celebrities
whose praises I could sing.

Opera singers, Jessye Norman, Kathleen Battle
and Leotyne Price,
Jordan Greenway, who plays hockey on ice,
the first Black player on the US Olympic team.
This young man is living his dream.
Musicians, Scott Joplin, Billy Holiday, Nina Simone,
Wynton Marsalis, Miles Davis and Quincy Jones.
Athletes Colin Kaepernick and Mohammad Ali
who had the courage and conviction of right
to fight for the way things ought to be.
We honor those brave Black men and women in service
to our country, and for our freedom,
and those who gave their lives
in service to others, the ultimate sacrifice,
I cannot name every Black person
who has made a contribution to the world,
and to our community,
for the greater good of our society,
So if the name of your favorite I did not mention,
please don't be offended, as that was not my intention.

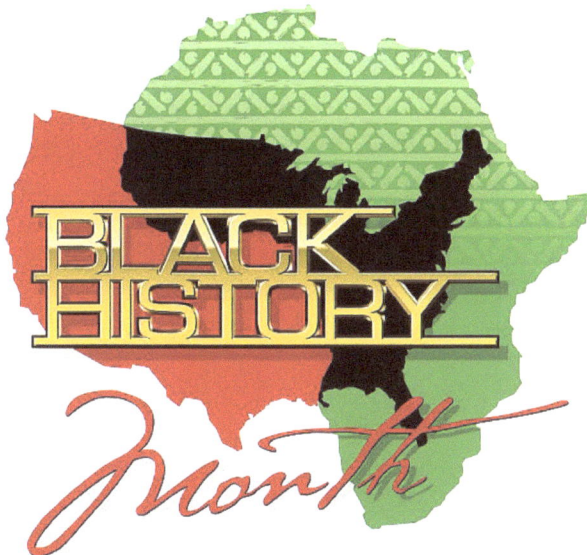

One Nation One People

The Martin Luther King Memorial in Washington DC
was unveiled and dedicated ceremoniously.
Inspired by his words from "I have a dream,"
near where memorials of Jefferson and Lincoln are seen,
a monument carved from a huge block of stone
depicts Martin Luther King standing alone.
"Out of a mountain of despair, a stone of hope"
brought forth this work of art,
a monument together with other great men,
yet also set apart.
For the struggle of civil rights it is a metaphor.
He worked to
make life better
for all people
not just his
own race,
but for people
from each and
every place.
From the top of
the steps in 1963
he made his plea
for racial equality,
symbolically
connecting us
together,
building a bridge
to demonstrate
how we are
one nation,
one people,
and the
time is now.

Statues and Statutes

Statues that glorify generals of the confederacy
have no place in American history.
They were traitors who, like #45 and his family
put wealth and greed
before the human rights and need
of every person for freedom and liberty,
and we should not honor their memory.
Lessons should be taught in history
of those who fought for victory,
but to have a sense of Southern Pride
for those who were on the losing side
leaves us all divided,
so that we cannot be united.
One nation is what we are supposed to be
in spite of differing philosophy.
You won't see statutes of Hitler in Germany
although they haven't forgotten their history.
No statues of dictators or flags or signs
outside of museums to remind
the citizens of what they all went through
in World War One and World War Two.
I feel for those who lost family members to war,
who had no choice but to fight for
their country of origin
or the state they lived within,
whether or not with the war they agreed,
or indeed, with the people who were the enemy
as they were told, either way, on war they were all sold.

"We won two world wars, beautiful world wars."

**- Donald Trump in a TV interview with
Chris Wallace on July 21, 2020**

Nasty Women

There are nasty women everywhere it seems
who often haunt poor Donald's dreams.
Strong women appear to frighten and intimidate,
so he would like to eliminate
them with name-calling and walking away
when the truth they begin to say,
or if there is a question he wants to avoid.
You don't have to have studied Freud
to understand he is emotionally immature,
a frightened boy and what is more,
of Kamala Harris he is terrified,
and so he has said she's not qualified,
and questions her parent's citizenship.
He's just on another ego trip.
He's rude to all good women, as far as I can tell,
yet in spite of all Ghislaine Maxwell's crimes,
to her, he wishes well!

Person, woman, man, camera, TV.
IQ45 can repeat this perfectly.
He thinks he got extra points for saying them in order,
I think his cognitive comprehension is south of the border.
His pronunciation is an abomination,
where is Yo Semite or Thigh Land?
Does he mean there are Black and Jewish people
living on Long Island?
He has been known to push more
to get his image on Mount Rushmore.
To be up there you need to have passed away,
a situation many would deem OK,
except for his image to be carved in stone,
that's an honor reserved alone
for people who have done great things, and deserved
to be remembered by history.
Not like him, who has only brought
disgrace, dishonor, and treachery.

Prayers for Malala

A teenage girl trying to be
a good example to her community;
trying to fight a culture
opposed to female education,
when in retaliation
this brave young girl was shot in the head
on her way home from school,
and left for dead.

This was an act beyond comprehension,
and the world should pay attention
to cries of oppressed females everywhere
who are treated in a way that is so unfair.
The world was outraged
that in this day and age
a child can be targeted
because she fights for equality.

Candlelight vigils, protests and prayer,
Malala's supporters were everywhere.
We all prayed that she
would make a complete recovery,
but we must never give up the fight
for a basic human right,
that girls and women in every nation
have the opportunity for education.

Now our prayers have been answered,
and Malala has achieved
more than anyone could have believed.
She has written a best-selling book,
met Her Majesty the Queen,
addressed the United Nations,

won a Nobel Peace Prize,
when she was only seventeen!
So God Bless Malala
and keep her in your care,
as she fights for the rights of girls
and women everywhere.

"I tell my story, not because it is unique, but because it is not. It is the story of many girls."
- Malala Yousafzai, Nobel Lecture, 2014 Peace Prize

Dreams of Martin Luther King

The dream and vision of Martin Luther King
was to see a future that would bring
people together of every race.
Let your community be the place
where dreams come true.
Ask yourself what you can do
and how you can be,
to make his dream a reality.
What does it take to reach out a hand
to help another, and to understand
that we are brothers and sisters underneath.
That color of skin, or religious belief
are outer differences; we are the same.
So when you hear the name of Dr. King,
ask yourself what you can bring
to your community to help it be
a place of racial harmony.
We are still building on his dream.
Over the years we have seen
progress made and barriers removed;
with people like Rosa Parks, whose bravery proved
that one person can change the status quo
to make a difference, and you know
that to make the dream real you have to feel
a bond with all people, and you have to see
that's it's all up to me, and it's all up to you
for Martin Luther King's dreams to all come true.

Rosa L Parks, an American activist in the civil rights movement.

"Karen"

Whether you're birdwatching in the park
or walking home alone in the dark
or selling bottled water or lemonade,
people of all ethnicities shouldn't be afraid
that an angry white woman will report you to the law,
and sometimes you're not even sure
what they are reporting you for.
These angry white women have been given a name
which seems to place the blame
on every woman who's name is the same.

Who chose the name Karen, as I'd like to know why?
And what about Felicia when we said bye?
I find it very hard to believe
that Felicia actually didn't leave.
I know women called Karen
who are not angry or mean,
so it doesn't really seem fair
that every Karen has to bear
the brunt of one woman who lost her mind
and said words that were very unkind.
We should call them "Ivankas" not "Karens"
as it seems to me
that name suits them perfectly!

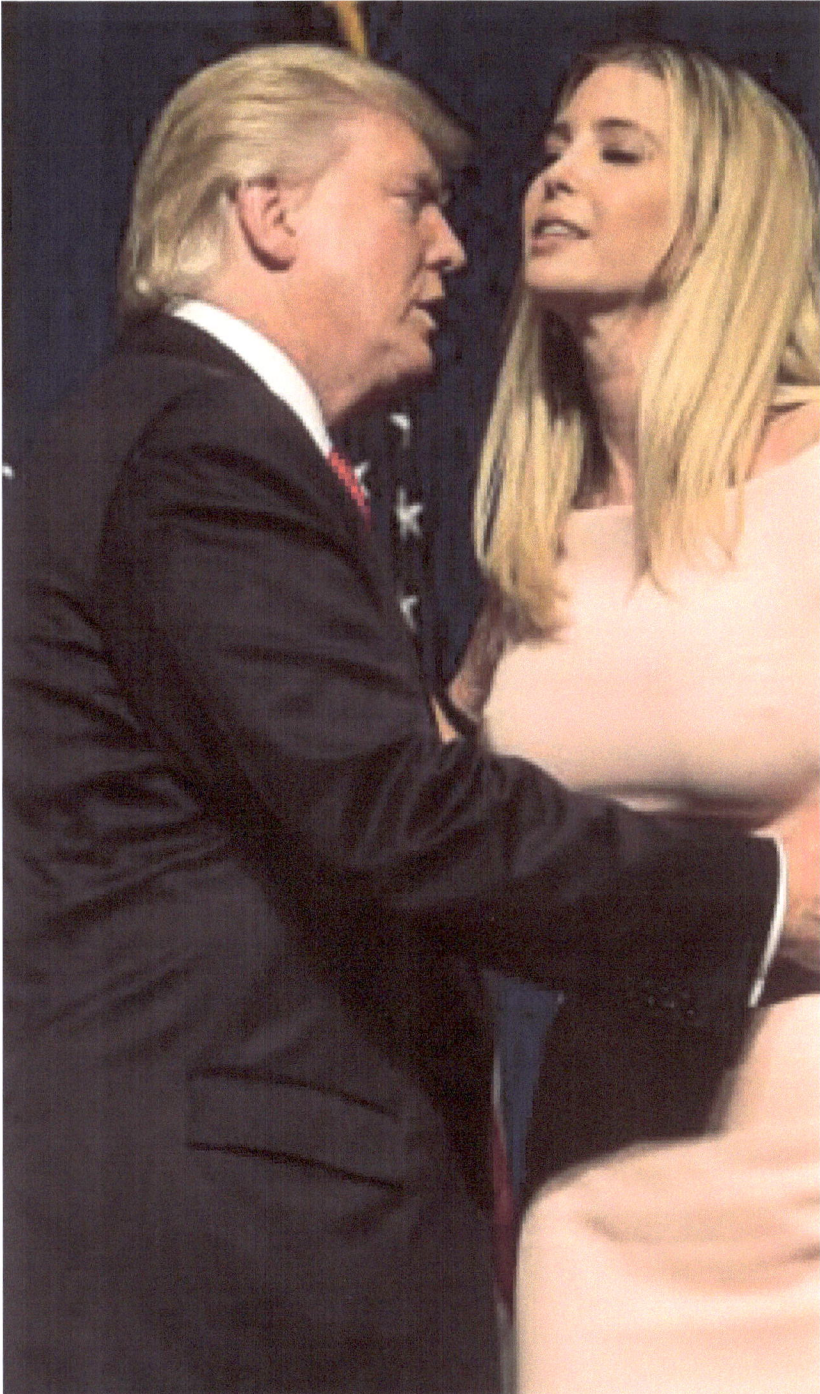

To Tell The Truth

At #45's impeachment Colonel Vindman testified
and now he has been vilified
by tRump and his band of thieves,
because he knows the world believes
that Colonel Vindman was telling the truth,
and soon the world will have the proof
to put #45 and his co-conspiriting traitors away,
and we hope they never see the light of day.

We know that #45 doesn't tell the truth
nor does he care about the safety of our youth,
or if children in school are shot
or if they catch the virus or not.
The immigrant children are in cages still
and he doesn't care that they probably will
catch the virus, and many will die
but not one tear will #45 cry.
All he cares about is to get reelected,
which we have long suspected.

He let Paul Manafort serve his sentence at home
as he's afraid to face the virus in prison alone.
Roger Stone's sentence he has commuted,
but not Michael Cohen, as he is reputed
to be writing a book that will tell all
and help to lead to #45's downfall.

And Ghislaine Maxwell, in jail she will stay
until the virus or "suicide" takes her away.
She was Epstein's Madam, young girls she procured
with promises of a modeling career or assured
them that they could be a star in movies or TV.
They were treated to a lavish lifestyle
that included sexual favors to the famous and rich,
so I hope that this bitch gets the
punishment she deserves for sure,
but I hope that before her end
she "spills the beans" on #45 and his friends.

Celebrating the Life of Martin Luther King Jr.

Born to a minister and his wife in 1929,
he started out his life as Michael Jr.,
until his father changed his name to Martin Luther
when they travelled to Germany in 1934,
the name of Michael King was no more.
The Protestant leader's memory inspired this choice,
and perhaps helped influence his theological voice.
King grew up in Atlanta and his progress was great;
skipping grades and leaving High School in 1948.
At the age of fifteen his college studies began.
He earned degrees in sociology and divinity by 1951,
and married Coretta Scott in 1953,
then went on to earn a Doctorate in Philosophy.
Now a Baptist minister and father of four,
King could tolerate segregation no more.
An activist and leader of Civil Rights,
and always non-violent in his fights.
Influenced by great leaders from the past
his crusade for justice had an impact that would last.
He led the bus boycott in Montgomery
and the march on Washington in 1963.
"I have a dream" was a speech he was famous for.
He fought to end poverty and the Vietnam war.
His words were analyzed and criticized
by both black and white,
but Martin Luther King continued
to fight the good fight.

He won the Nobel Prize in 1964,
no-one that young had ever won it before.
He went to Memphis in April of 1968,
in spite of threats against him, which had been great.
After his prophetic "mountaintop" speech was done
outside his room in the late afternoon sun,
he was shot on the second-floor balcony
of the Lorraine Motel, in Memphis, Tennessee.
His dying request to a musician was assured,
who later that night played
"Take my Hand Precious Lord."
Many years have passed since he's been gone,
but his message of hope and truth keeps marching on.
Let us all be participants of the team
as we move towards the fulfillment of his dream.

"I Have A Dream.."

Rev. Dr. Martin Luther King Jr.

In Memory of Maya

Born Marguerite Johnson in 1928,
her brother gave her the nickname of Maya.
Her childhood was horrific,
but like a phoenix rising from the fire
a terrific genius was born.
Raped by her mother's boyfriend at the age of eight,
she told her brother who reported the crime,
but the guilty man served only one day of time.
He was killed when he was released from the jail cell,
and she thought he would have lived if she didn't tell.
She thought it was her fault that he was dead,
so for five years not a word she said,
and living silently alone in her head.
Observing the world around her and reading constantly,
and developing an incredible memory.
She credits a teacher, Bertha Flowers,
a woman who spent many hours
introducing her to Shakespeare,
Dickens and Edgar Allen Poe,
and also Black authors, both male and female, and so
from these silent years came her yearning
to experience many kinds of learning.
At age 23 she married a Greek man in 1951,
although at the time interracial marriage
was frowned upon.
At the Purple Onion night club
she performed using the name of Rita,
but her mangers thought that
Maya Angelou sounded much sweeter,
as she sang and danced in Calypso style,
which she did for quite a while.
Then Maya studied dance with
Martha Graham and Alvin Ailey,

performing Porgy and Bess she travelled Europe with an
opera company and taking the opportunity
to learn the language of each country.
She worked as a dancer, an actress, a singer, a cook
before she had published her very first book.
She wrote autobiographies, lyrics and plays
a prolific writer of poetry and essays.
She was an actor, composer, director,
producer of movies and films for TV.
The scope of her work is humbling to me.
A renaissance woman with a mellifluous voice
ahead of her time, living the life of her choice.
A teacher, a friend and advisor of political leaders
from many nations.
Maya received over fifty honorary degrees,
many medals, honors and awards,
including three Grammys,
a Tony and a Pulitzer nomination.
A friend and mentor to Oprah Winfrey,
both role models for women
who showed that no matter
the circumstances of your youth,
great things can be achieved if you live your own truth.

"The caged bird sings
with a fearful trill
of things unknown
but longed for still
and his tune is heard
on the distant hill
for the caged bird
sings of freedom."

Kids in Cages

Whatever happened to all those kids in cages?
We haven't heard anything about them for ages.
How many died from Covid 19?
We haven't heard and we haven't seen
anything on the Internet or in the newspapers.
How many were abused by guards and child rapers?

Why is this happening in the USA?
How can we turn a blind eye and say
that their parents should have come here legally,
or endured the problems of their own country?

Why would so many people risk life and limb
to come to a country on a whim?
They must have faced a life or death situation
to want to come to this God forsaken nation,
where they are punished for wanting to be free
in the so-called "land of liberty."

What did your ancestors come here for,
were they fleeing famine, pestilence or war?
Or because they thought life would be better here,
and that they could finally live without any fear?

And those who claim that their ancestors came
on ships from Spain, England or France,
seeking religious freedom and the chance
for better lives for their families.

Some ancestors were brought here against their will
forced to work for masters who still
try to keep their descendants under oppression
by suppressing freedom of expression.

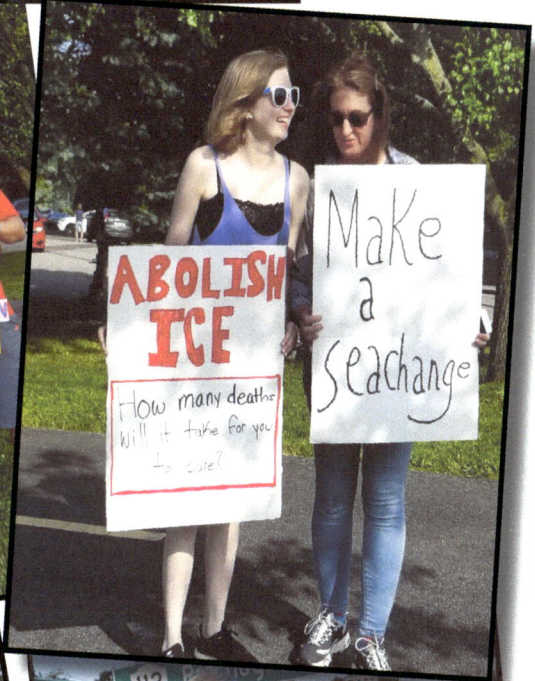

Tik Tok

Tik Tok, tRump was in shock,
when he found out that punked he'd been
by teenagers, who were nowhere to be seen
in the thousands of arena seats which were bare,
there was nobody sitting there.
The teens had ordered tickets
they never planned to use.
Now #45 with his very short fuse
will twitter away his dismay.
When they heard tRumps's rally play
"I Won't Stand Down,"
the fans of Tom Petty were wearing a frown.
His family and estate were really pissed
and issued an order to cease and desist.
They don't want it used at a rally for hate,
so they didn't hesitate
to send notification of their legal intent,
to the illegitimate president.
There are more than a dozen artists who protested
the use of their famous songs
by a party that promotes
ideologies that are wrong.
Adele, The O'Jays and Neil Young
don't want their music to be sung.
The Rolling Stones, Elton John,
Aerosmith, Earth Wind and Fire,
all say that they have no desire
for their songs to be played
at a tRump rally, and were dismayed
that even though their permission was denied,
as usual tRump's people lied
and played their music anyway.

Flags and Rags

Swastikas and confederate flags
have no place in this land.
Why can't people understand
that wars were fought, and many people died
fighting against slavery and genocide,
so that we can live peacefully
in the land of the free.
Yet some people still display
these symbols of hatred today.
They don't even seem to care
that to see them flying there
opens wounds of ancestral pain,
feelings that will still remain.
These offensive emblems represent
the defeated flag of our opponents.
Those who fly the flags of the enemy
must be traitors, it seems to me.

"I refuse to believe that Southern pride stems from the pain we've inflicted on others. Southern pride comes from what we've built together. In our music and art and innovation..."

— Jason Latour, Comic Book Artist

Still Striving Together

In 1968 there was a climate of hate
in certain parts of the USA,
and we have to wonder
is it that much different today?
Over fifty years later how much have we progressed
towards the end of human unrest?
As some of us strive for equality
there are others who embrace negativity.
For every step forward there is another step back,
as though we are running on a moving track.
If Martin Luther King were alive today
what do you think he would have to say
of the prejudice towards people who are refugees,
fleeing from danger in war torn countries?
The times we live in are dark indeed.
So many people who don't have what they need
in order to survive, or merely stay alive.

"When I give food
to the poor,
they call me a saint.

When I ask why the
poor have no food,
they call me a
communist."

Dom Helder Camara

The basic lessons that all prophets taught,
was that as human beings we ought
to treat our neighbors with love and care,
and to help other people everywhere.
As a minister Rev. King's philosophy
was one of Christian charity.
Racism, bigotry and homophobia
were not the values that
Martin Luther King stood for.
But feeding the hungry, helping the poor,
building bridges not walls, and opening every door,
by building people up, not tearing them down,
as there is no place for bullying in our town,
or for that matter in any place
as we are all part of the human race.
So let us strive for a future that will bring
the dreams and vision of the
Rev. Dr. Martin Luther King.

Inter-Faith Understanding

Christians, Jews, Sikhs, Muslims and Baha'is
and people of all faiths who realize
that through understanding our religious philosophies
our differences are fewer than our similarities.

People from all countries and religious denominations
coming together as united nations
to show solidarity with one another,
to show that we are all sisters and brothers
of one supreme spirit who loves us all,
no matter by what name we call
the father and mother of the universe.

So when one of our
brothers commits an act so perverse
as to kill innocent people because of their belief,
we mourn for those lost
and cry out in grief,
yet our faith teaches forgiveness,
as difficult as it may be
to love all members of society.

It is time now to heal the wounds of the past
and educate people so they know at last
that for this world to truly be free
we must respect each other's culture and history.

Mosiac copy of Norman Rockwell's
painting The Golden Rule at the UN Building in NY

It Is What It Is

When asked about the virus by the press
tRump showed no empathy, and didn't express
any words of sympathy to the people losing their families,
their incomes, their homes, their businesses,
all he can say is, "it is what it is."

But the MyPillow guy was asked by Don the Con
to invent a drug they could both profit from.
He asked him to make sure
that he would find a miracle cure.
So on Anderson Cooper's show
the MyPillow guy just had to go
to foster sales of his drug of choice,
but Anderson Cooper didn't give him his voice.

Cooper said it is snake oil that he is selling
and lies to the public he is telling;
that the Better Business Bureau doesn't endorse
his products as they are fraudulent, of course.
The MyPillow guy said he does it to glorify the Lord,
but he didn't say that he's on the board
of the company that makes
the drug he is promoting,
and talks about it on TV gloating
of how he gave it to all his friends and family.
Will they still get Covid? We shall see.

---

*"It's an absolute miracle, I take it every
day. I don't get the virus."*

- MyPillow Guy, Mike Lindell

Chaska, MN
12:17 PM CT

PANDEMIC
GLOBALLY
TOTAL CASES   DEATHS
21,943,183   775,439
IN THE UNITED STATES
TOTAL CASES   DEATHS
5,454,333   170,905
SOURCE: JOHNS HOPKINS UNIVERSITY

TONIGHT ON CNN
DEMOCRATIC
NATIONAL
CONVENTION
BILL CLINTON

LIVE

CORONAVIRUS PANDEMIC
"MYPILLOW" CREATOR: TRUMP "ENTHUSIASTIC" OVER UNPROVEN THERAPEUTIC
Mike Lindell | Board Member of Phoenix BioTech, which produces Oleandrin   NAS ▲ 69.95
OVER THE WEEKEND, DEATH VALLEY REACHED RECORD-BREAKING 130°   ► NEWSROOM

The Divine Spirit

The divine spirit, or force, is in every human soul
we are part of it, it is part of us,
and is what makes us whole.
Many gods have many names,
but they are all one and the same,
for all religions were created by man,
there has been some form of religion since
human life began.

Some built idols of wood or rock and stone,
as nobody wants to face the world alone.
Some worshiped the moon, the stars, and the sun,
and prayed for good fortune from everyone.
Some created mythical gods with fanciful stories
of battles and lovers, defeats, and glories.

Now we make idols of rock stars, or of a king or queen,
and stars of TV and the silver screen.
We idolize musicians of all sorts,
political leaders or stars of sports.
There is a human need to idolize,
to worship something greater,
but we must realize that this is a gift from our creator.

For the real power of God is within our reach,
which is what all the prophets tried to teach.
If we follow the teachings of enlightened souls
whose lessons help us reach life's goals,
we all have the potential to be one with the spirit divine,
the choice is really yours and mine.
The whole world is our sister and brother,
when we are one with God and each other.

BLM Fifth Ave.

Black Lives Matter painted on Fifth Avenue
by Black and Hispanic men who
were wrongly accused
of a rape in Central Park many years ago,
when tRump took out an ad
in the NY Times to say that he believed
that the death penalty they should receive.
But years later they were released from jail
as DNA evidence failed to show
that any of them were guilty, and so
it is poetic justice for tRump to know
that they helped to paint those words of power
right in front of his tRump Tower.
Now how much better will it be
when #45's abode
is on President Barack Obama Road!

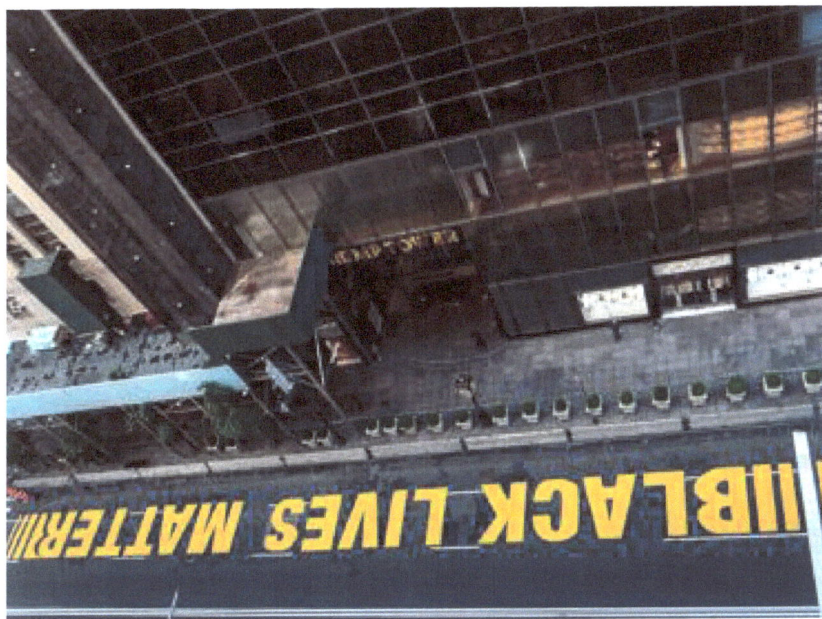

The "Write" Stuff

Bob Woodward, who helped reveal Nixon's crimes,
and David Enrich of the New York Times,
have both written books that are exposés
of Donald Trump's criminal ways.

Woodward's latest book is entitled "Rage,"
and it held my interest on every page.
Enrich's book is about the Deutsche Bank.
It is those "money managers" that we have to thank
for enabling #45 to get away for so long
with financial decisions that were all wrong.
"Disloyal" is the name of Michael Cohen's book,
who exposes tRump for the crook
we always knew him to be,
it just confirms the depth of his treachery.

"The Room Where it Happened," John Bolton's book,
had tRump and his cohorts all shook up.
They tried to stop publication
but can't fool everyone in the nation.
Many books on the best seller list
tell the true stories of how voters missed
the opportunity of a good president, because
they didn't enforce the emoluments clause.

Mary's book tells the family story of dysfunction,
and she has no compunction to withhold the
mashed potatoes story, that was told
and angered Donald
when his sister said,
remember when his brother
Fred dumped a bowl
of mashed potatoes on his head!

RAGE
BOB WOODWARD

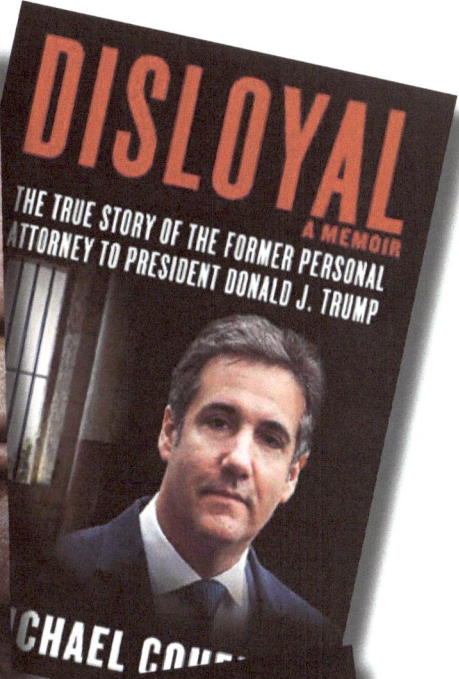

DISLOYAL
A MEMOIR
THE TRUE STORY OF THE FORMER PERSONAL
ATTORNEY TO PRESIDENT DONALD J. TRUMP

MICHAEL COHEN

THE
ROOM
WHERE IT
HAPPENED

A White House Memoir

JOHN
BOLTON

Former National Security Advisor
of the United States

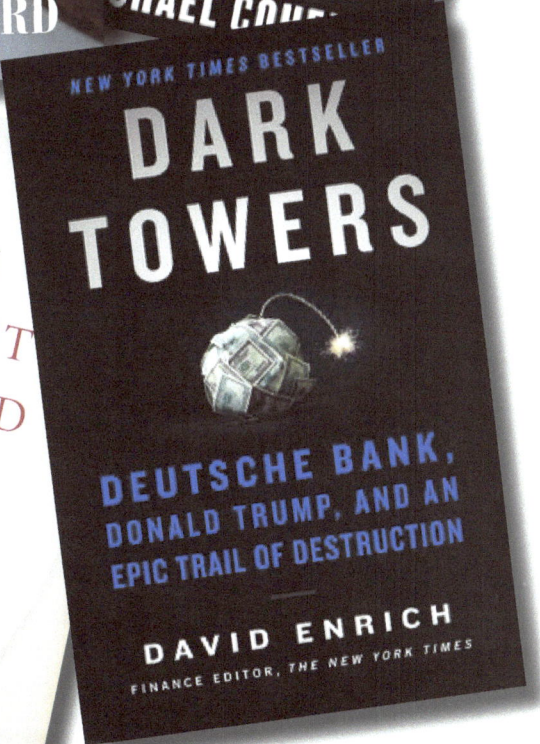

NEW YORK TIMES BESTSELLER

**DARK
TOWERS**

DEUTSCHE BANK,
DONALD TRUMP, AND AN
EPIC TRAIL OF DESTRUCTION

DAVID ENRICH
FINANCE EDITOR, THE NEW YORK TIMES

Though The Eyes of Youth

Through the eyes of youth
the legacy of truth must march on.
For future generations
must know the tribulations
of those who went before.
As those who forget the past
will never be free at last,
but will be doomed to repeat
the patterns of defeat for evermore.
What kind of world will future generations inherit?
Will it be one of unified merit,
or will we still be judging on ethnicity
and fearful of diversity?
Over the years this country has seen
people of many backgrounds who have been
persecuted because of the color of their skin,
or their native origin;
African, Irish, Japanese,
and now an influx of refugees.
Do we live by the words on the Statue of Liberty,
"Give me your poor yearning to be free,"
or do we reject them out of fear,
and say we don't want their kind here?
With prayerful, peaceful demonstration,
not angry mobs of devastation
is how injustice is overcome,
and peaceful co-existence is won.
We must teach our children, so they understand
the non-violent protests are what Dr. King planned,
following the philosophy of his theology,
to love your enemies, as hard as it may seem,
yet is the only way to fulfill the Rev. Dr.'s dream.

In Memory of Congressman John Lewis

A quiet warrior was he,
a man who will go down in history
as a hero who fights for civil rights.
He was just a student when
he sat at lunch counters
with other young Black men
to try to break the color bar,
which took a long time before
they got very far.
He was beaten, arrested
and tear-gassed
many times before
the Civil Rights Act was passed.
Lewis marched with Martin Luther King
and believed in non-violent protesting.
Respected by both parties he was known
as the "conscience of Congress,"
who stood alone.
A freedom fighter for more than fifty years,
his loss is cause for many tears.
As he lay in state three past presidents paid
their respects and gave thanks
for the positive changes that he made
helping Black people who lived in places remote,
and encouraging them to register to vote.
"You can redeem the soul of the nation," said John.
His legacy of hope will carry on.

For the very last time over a bridge in Selma,
named for a racist notorious,
John Lewis found his eternal rest,
his mission in life, victorious.

photo Courtesy of the office of Congressman Tom Suozzi

The Truth Shall Set You Free

Some say God is black, some say God is white,
some may feel God's presence
in the darkness of the night.
Some say God's a He, some say God's a She,
other people have no gender for their deity.
Who's to say who's wrong?
Who's to say who's right?
For what's true is all the above,
the truth is God is love.
Some people pray all day, and other people pray
only when their life seems not to go their way.
Some give thanks when things go right.
Some ask for help and hope God might
change the course their life is taking,

and turn to him in fright.
Who's to say who's wrong?
Who's to say who's right?
For what's true is all the above,
the truth is God is love.
Some think a house of worship
is important to their prayer,
they find comfort in the ritual, others do not care
to make church going habitual,
yet find God's presence everywhere.
Some people are uplifted
by the pomp and circumstance,
others express their love of God
through their music and their dance.
Who's to say who's wrong?
Who's to say who's right?
For what's true is all the above,
the truth is God is love.

About The Author

Victoria Crosby is a journalist, writing for newspapers and magazines for more than twenty years. Her motivational and inspirational poetry has been featured in many publications, and on her weekly radio show, Oasis. Her political satire poetry column, Per-Verse, was featured in the now defunct Long Island Voice, an offshoot of The Village Voice.

She has also written the life story, in rhyming verse, of Elvis Presley, which is featured on WHPC 90.3, twice a year on the anniversary of his birth and death. She performs her humorous and inspirational poetry for many groups and she performs her Elvis, Frank Sinatra, and other celebrities life story poetry with singers, as part of a group called "Poetry in Motion."

As Poet Laureate for the City of Glen Cove since 1994, she has written and read at many special occasions, for individuals and organizations in Glen Cove, and the Long Island community at large. Victoria is on the board of many non-profit organizations, including the Historic Royal Palaces in the UK and the Glen Cove Arts Council, a charity she founded in 2006

Born and raised in Cheshire, UK, with elementary and high school education in England, educator and music teacher Victoria Crosby received her Master's Degree from Long Island University.

Also by Victoria Crosby...

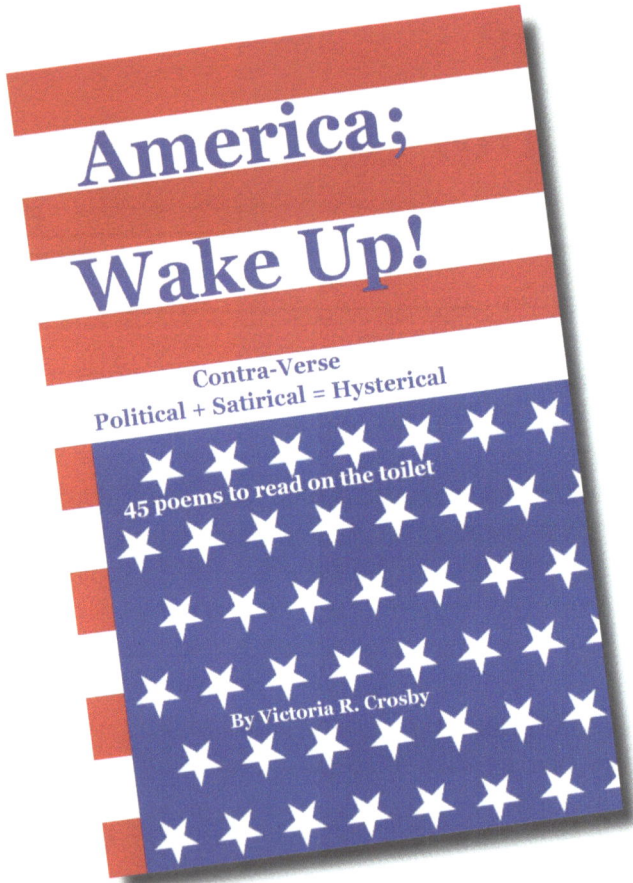

"America; Wake Up!"

Sometimes you have to laugh to keep from crying. This is why we need political satire, to laugh and cry at human foibles. Written by an acclaimed poet and journalist, whose work ranges from humorous to inspirational, and who, as a political activist herself, has supported many humanitarian causes. With quotes and tweets from philosophers, religious leaders, writers, presidents and dictators, and photographs on topics from the serious to the absurd, this poetry collection chronicles the years 2016-2019 in rhyming verse.

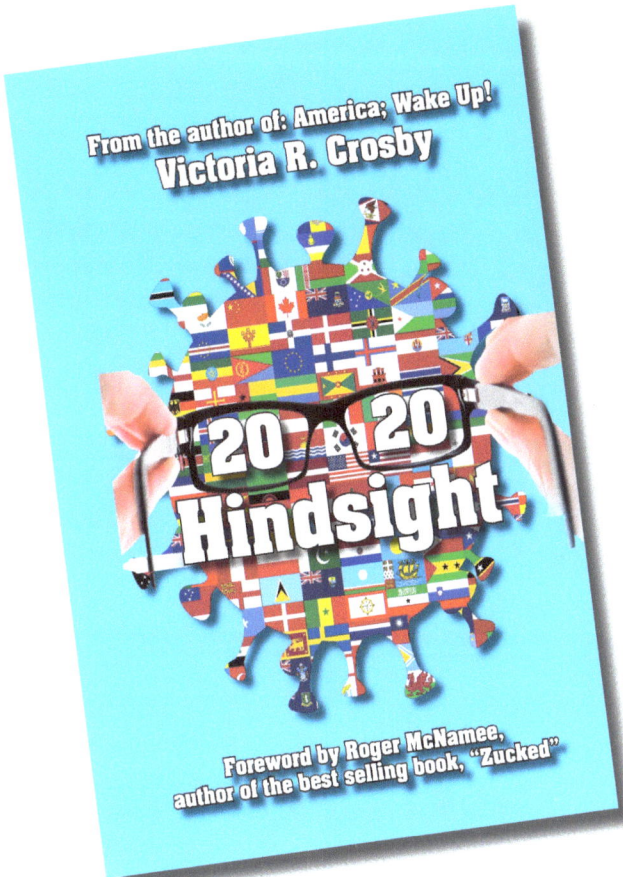

Poetry for a Pandemic

Victoria R. Crosby hadn't planned on writing another political poetry book, however, after staying at home due to the Corona Virus, more poems were inevitable.

These poems are anger in action, inspired by the incompetence and continued mismanagement of the virus crisis by the current US administration.

Victoria uses the power of the pen, or in this case the keyboard, to express her outrage, once again using satirical humor, photos and quotes from the famous and the infamous. 2020 Hindsight was written in March and April of 2020, so Victoria takes no responsibility for any insanity that probably will occur during the following months of the year.

www.ingramcontent.com/pod-product-compliance
Lightning Source LLC
Chambersburg PA
CBHW051238090426
42742CB00001B/6